AF579687

Bad Penny
And Other Short Stories

By Tamara Rice

Dedicated to Melissa for her encouragement and to Bryn for begging me to write something he would finally be allowed to read.

Table of Contents

The Garden Hose

The garden hose resided on a metal garden hose hanger attached to the back of a tidy house in a tidy neighborhood, as so many garden hoses do. Her life was pretty uneventful for the most part. Once or twice a week The Wife would take her down to water her plants. Occasionally there would be a dry spell and The Husband would take her down to water the lawn. It was a good life as life goes for garden hoses.

She observed all manner of backyard wildlife while carefully coiled on her hanger. The birds bouncing along the grass seeking their next meal. The chipmunks scurrying in and out of their hidey holes. She made friends with them in her mind. She was content.

One day a garter snake appeared and discovered the flat rock next to the garden shed. It was warmed by the sun and he decided it was the perfect spot to lounge. The garden hose had never seen such a lovely creature. She was stunned by his beauty and for the first time in her life she regretted being a garden hose. This made her feel silly and more than a little embarrassed.

"Stop being foolish," she thought to herself. *"You are a garden hose and your purpose in life is to water things. Not moon about over lovely creatures."*

But she couldn't stop. Every sunny day he returned to the rock and every time she loved him more. Long after she thought it was even possible to.

One midsummer afternoon when it was too hot for him to claim his rock the neighbor's children took her down to play hot day water games. They soaked each other and squealed with laughter. They used their thumbs to create a fine spray in which they could admire the rainbows. When they were done they turned off the spigot but left her sprawled unceremoniously in the grass as they raced back home for ice pops.

As night came she dreamed. Garden

hoses don't truly sleep but their minds wander. She felt the grass and imagined that she was also a lovely creature and he would welcome her on his rock. She was ashamed but was powerless against those thoughts. She knew she would never be anything but a garden hose yet her imagination told her otherwise.

As the sun rose and the early morning hours passed her mind continued to drift. So much so that she was startled from her dreaming by the garter snake crossing her back as he headed to his rock. She had never felt such joy! She knew he didn't really see her but for one shining moment he was aware she existed. That was enough.

There is no fairytale happy ending. One sunny day he didn't appear and he never appeared again. She didn't know if he had found a nicer rock in a different yard or if he had a tragic encounter with a lawnmower. Her heart broke at the latter thought so she convinced herself that he was happier somewhere else.

Over the years other garter snakes found the rock but they were not him so she paid them no mind. The Wife died so the garden hose was no longer taken down to water plants. The Husband was so sad that he stopped caring if the lawn got dry. The neighbor's kids were grown so there were no more hot day water games.

Her hanger rusted, her coating cracked from age and the elements, but still her heart sang with love. For one shining moment he was aware she existed.

Dreaming

In her dream she is only wearing one shoe. Waves of panic wash over her as she tries to remember where the missing shoe could be. She can't look for it because that would mean stopping. She doesn't dare take the time but can she afford not to? Her bare right foot leaves behind bloody tracks that could give away her position. To whom? She doesn't even know anymore.

On some level she knows she is dreaming. She always does but it never changes anything. The fear is real every time. She's not screaming in her head to wake up. Not yet.

The building changes. It's a house now but one she doesn't recognize. It's dark and unfamiliar so it slows her down a little. From what she can make out it appears to be a nice house. Why are there stairs missing, though? How can that be safe for the toddler that lives there? She briefly wonders why she assumed children lived there before entering the toy strewn hallway. Her mind is just filling it in as she goes along now. Naturally the hall is too long. It always is. The sensation of being pursued grows stronger. Just stay out of the bedrooms. That's where the bad stuff happens.

Suddenly it's a kitchen but not a kitchen. There's a sink and a refrigerator on her right but it's still part of the hallway. The freezer and refrigerator doors are ajar. She tries to quickly close both but something's stopping them. She won't look. She's not stupid enough to look but she tries to force them shut because it feels important. Her attempts are fruitless, though, and someone or something is still coming for her so she moves on.

It's getting harder to see but she senses that her bloody footprints are still visible in her wake. If only she had taken a moment to put her shoe on the other foot. It may have made her harder to follow. She may have been able to finally make her way to safety. It was always somehow her fault.

There it is. She finds herself in a bedroom anyway. She never entered a door, it was just waiting at the end of the hallway. She should have known. She makes out the shape of a wooden dining room chair and tries her best to crouch behind it as the dark figure on the bed sits up. Whatever was pursuing her stops. Their purpose wasn't to harm her themselves but to drive her towards the one who would. She's trapped and the screaming in her head begins.

She Always Had Your Back

When she was 6 or 7 years old she was sitting in the back seat of the car when her mother suddenly pointed to a driveway as they passed and said,"J.D. Salinger lives there but you must never tell anyone."

"I won't," she assured her.

She had no idea at that time who J. D. Salinger was but she was prepared to take his secret to the grave with her. She started reading young and would voraciously consume any book she could get her hands on but her family wasn't exactly into the classics. With the exception of Little Women, most of what she read was a combination of Nancy Drew books from the school library and any crap horror novel she came across at home. The sorts of books that involved the ghostly dead brutally murdering the living, cockroach swarms that ate young couples having sex in the back of pickup trucks, and even one about modern day Amazons that, in hindsight, was clearly some incel's graphic rape fantasy. Real classy shit.

But her mind had many questions about it all. Was he hiding from the authorities or just people in general? The subject had never come up before but would strangers now sense that she possessed this information and ask her? What if it was someone she knew? Should she keep it secret from them, as well? She had a lot of experience with keeping secrets and hiding information from the outside world but this gave her one more thing to worry about. What if the people looking for him were bad and tortured her? What if she revealed his location by accident? She had no clue who this human was but desperately wanted to protect him because it felt important in a way she couldn't explain.

She never got around to reading Catcher In the Rye until 10th grade English class. She didn't love it but remembered that mental promise she made to him years before. He died in 2010 and she was never put in the position where she had to fork over that information. It was one of those meaningless childhood fears, like the danger of quicksand. But even under threat of pain she would not have given up that secret. After all, she was a young child and had already forgotten where they were by the time they made it a half a mile down the road.

Valentine's Day

The three young women entered room 2 and Sarah immediately spotted the empty condom box on the floor. "Someone had a good weekend," she laughed. Janet pointed out that it was only a 3 pack and not the 12 pack so did they really? The silly banter continued as they went from room to room picking up the tips that would be pooled and distributed at the end of the shift. It was the Monday morning after Valentine's Day and every room had been occupied over the weekend.

Janet was only two years older than Sarah and three more than Tina but, as was often the case in her life, she simply didn't blend. She didn't party with them after work or commiserate about overbearing parents. She was already on her third lifetime and her main concern in that moment was worrying that they would notice she was still in yesterday's clothes. She didn't need to feel more awkward and out of place than she already did but they were too overwhelmed by the mountain of work ahead of them to notice what she looked like.

She started on the bathroom in room 4 and tried to focus. Scrubbing it clean wasn't hard but hair was the devil. The room could sparkle and then a goddamn hair would magically appear in a spot that she knew she had already cleaned. How the hell would a pubic hair get down behind the toilet anyway? She could change a bed, wipe down all the antique furniture, and vacuum in the time it would take her to locate and remove every last hair from a bathroom.

On to room 7, the fanciest room. It was an upscale inn as it was but someone's significant other thought they were worth the extra expense. Someone was loved here. Maybe it was a romantic surprise or an anniversary. They didn't have to spend the night trying to sleep with a toddler on their sister's living room floor to give their drunken partner a chance to sober off and hopefully calm down.

Janet stripped the bed and tried to ignore the anxiety that was tying her stomach in knots. She had no idea what kind of shitstorm she was going to face when she finally made it back home. Maybe he would be sorry? But she knew from experience that that was just wishful thinking. He was never sorry and everything was always her fault. The question was really just how angry would he still be? It was her fault for making him angry but, even worse, it was her fault for scooping up their child and running to the neighbors. It was her fault for thinking he would calm down. She begged them not to call the police. To just let her and her baby sit there and be safe until he calmed down but then he was pounding at their door and bellowing threats and they had no choice.

The officers were angry with her, too. She refused to press charges so they thought she was wasting their time. They lectured her and told her that if this occurred again after July first that she would no longer have a choice. After that the law would go into effect that visible signs of abuse would result in arrest regardless of what the victim said so she may as well press charges. She wouldn't budge. She understood their frustration but they didn't understand hers. If she let them bring him in he would be out in a matter of hours even more angry than he was before. How could that be in the best interest of her and their child? How in hell would that make them safer? She didn't call them. She didn't want them to be called. But they kept him outside while she quickly collected what her baby would need so the officers could transport them both to her sister's for the night.

She hoped to avoid her bosses as she walked back to the linens room to grab more sheets. She had slipped straight upstairs when she came in because she wasn't ready to deal with them, yet. They were good people and she dreaded having to disappoint them. They didn't deserve to suffer consequences for her poor life choices but it had become unavoidable. Her car was a '92 Geo Storm that had been in the shop for a week and would likely be there a few weeks more or maybe forever because she couldn't afford the repairs. Her sister let her borrow her car to get to work that day but that wasn't a sustainable option. She had been using her husband's truck but she had no idea what the future would bring now. Besides, she couldn't manage to keep all these balls in the air any longer. It was a miracle that she hadn't completely fallen apart already. At the end of her shift she would tell them about the car and that she couldn't come back.

Janet and Sarah completed their rooms at roughly the same time and pitched in to help Tina finish her last. She was the youngest and a bit slower but she tried her best. They divided up the tips, which were underwhelming. Clearly the other two had hoped the holiday would make people more generous but Janet didn't care. Another five or ten bucks wasn't going to fix her mess of a life.

Janet took a deep breath and headed down to the front desk to speak with Gail. She explained about her car and how she couldn't come back. She apologized for not being able to give a proper notice and braced herself for an angry response. Instead Gail spotted her throat and burst into tears. She was old enough to understand what the marks meant. Janet didn't know what to do so she just stood there and let Gail hold her. She never knew how to react when others displayed more distress over her life than she did. Once Gail calmed down they said their goodbyes. As she left Janet glanced at the vase full of roses that Gail had proudly displayed on the desk for everyone to admire. She was glad. Gail deserved to have a happy Valentine's Day.

Normal

She wasn't entirely sure but she believed the revolt began with her eyebrows. For many years she did what was expected of her. She carefully attempted to tweeze them into what others would determine to be a pleasing shape. She even got them waxed a couple times. If her brows looked like they were properly maintained then maybe, just maybe, people would believe she was normal. She did her best to be considerate. She taught her children to share. She gave money to the men standing at intersections holding their signs that reminded her that even though she didn't have much she still had enough to maybe buy them a meal. Or a bottle of wine. Whatever could give them some peace for a couple hours. Why should the configuration of the hair growing above her eyes matter in the grand scheme of things? Fuck her eyebrows.

Moving away from the makeup was a harder habit to break. It began with the blue mascara in the 80s. Everyone was doing it so she should, too. Maybe, just maybe, people would believe she was normal. Normal girls teased their hair and bought wet *n* wild lipstick and looked like they didn't hate themselves. They went to the mall and ate at the food court and talked about boys. She didn't care much for boys. She was pursued by the men who said they didn't like makeup on girls but only paid attention to the girls who wore it so she did. Over the years she continued to wear it to prove that having children didn't mean that a woman had to 'let herself go'. Her hair and face were as carefully made up as those of the other mothers at the playgroup. They thought she was normal, just like they were. As time went on the creative eye shadow looks were replaced by a quick swipe of blush over the lids to keep her from looking quite so washed out. Then it was down to just mascara so she wouldn't look so goddamn tired. But she *was* tired. Her son was the first male student to be the recipient of the Citizenship Award at 8th grade graduation. She was the mom taxi transporting a car full of geeks to wherever they needed to go. Did it matter if her face was painted? Fuck makeup.

She wore the off-the-shoulder tops when they were in. And the miserably uncomfortable hip huggers when it was their turn. If she wore what was in fashion then maybe, just maybe, people would believe she was normal. The long bell bottoms whose cuffs were caught beneath the heels of her boots and torn to shreds in the mud. The crop tops. The tank tops under flannel. When her son came home from school broken by his history class she showed him how to use Charity Navigator to find the best related causes to donate to. She spent countless hours arranging and discarding possible therapies for her disabled daughter. She supported her friends who were also struggling with what little emotional energy she had left. They didn't care if she wore pajama pants and baggy tees. Fuck real clothes. Maybe, just maybe, it didn't matter if people believed she was normal or not.

When the World Turned Funny

Justin sat on his bedroom floor and tried to pretend he couldn't hear the sound of angry yelling coming from downstairs. It scared him and he didn't want to be scared of his dad. His dad was his hero. He used to come home from work and take him out back to toss a ball or a frisbee. He said it helped him unwind, whatever that meant. Ever since the world turned funny he just comes home to shout at the people talking on TV. Last week at recess his friend Noah told him that his dad had started drinking beer and shouting at his mom so he knew it could be worse.

He looked at the toy cars on his shelf and wished he could play with them. Especially the pink Cadillac Fleetwood. That was his favorite. He thought boys weren't supposed to like pink things but his dad laughed and told him that was bullshit (but not to tell his mom that he used the word 'bullshit'). Now it just made him sad. The last time he tried to play with it, it got so hot that it started to burn his hand. He used a dirty sock to carefully put it back and didn't tell his parents because he didn't want to upset them again. When he told them about how his clock started running backwards his father only sighed but his mom went into the kitchen to cry. His mom cried a lot since the world turned funny.

He supposed he could do his homework while he waited for supper but it was only Friday afternoon. He would have plenty of time over the weekend. Besides, it wouldn't take him long now that the world turned funny. It was just some coloring pages and simple spelling words he already did last year in first grade. He remembered the look on Mrs. Blanc's face when she announced it was time for Social Studies and the book on her desk threw itself into the trash can. Her real smile was replaced by the kind of plastic smile he saw people use sometimes when they really didn't want their picture taken and she suggested they color pictures of the flag, instead. They colored a lot of pictures of the flag these days. No one complained, though. Especially after what happened to Emma. One day Emma asked Mrs. Blanc what something called 'rovey wait' was and her voice stopped working. Mrs. Blanc said Emma's mom homeschools her now. He missed Emma. She used to share her fruit snacks sometimes.

He realized his mom was calling him down for supper. He jumped up excitedly because it was Friday night and Friday night supper meant steak and steak was his favorite. The only thing he didn't like was that she still insisted on cutting it for him. He wasn't a baby anymore, he was a whole seven and a half years old but she kept saying that maybe he could try when he was eight. He sat down at the table and eyed his plate as his mouth watered. Steak, potatoes, and green beans. Perfect. He stabbed a piece of meat and brought it up to his mouth when suddenly he realized the steak disappeared. It was gone from the other plates, too. He looked up at his mother and noticed the tears in her eyes as she silently turned to dish them up some more potatoes.

Classy

They didn't have a designated smoking area so she stood around the corner in the sunny alley. The summer evening weather could not have been more perfect. She was sure the organizers must be delighted. A well dressed man joined her, standing several feet away and lit one up. They exchanged polite nods and for the millionth time that day she wondered if she made the right decision on her wardrobe. She knew nothing about fashion but thought the powder blue B. Moss dress should be appropriate. Her shoulders and upper back felt exposed but it didn't cling anywhere or show any cleavage. It fell just above her knee, though. Was that appropriate for a small town art gallery fundraiser? She didn't know and had no one to ask. The cheap dress flats were already hurting her feet.

She knew as much about art as she

did about fashion which was simply that she liked what she liked. The fliers had caught her attention only because she had begun to question if she should become more involved in the community. Especially since she had moved into the fancy house up on the hill. Her neighbors were the sort who joined garden clubs and attended fundraisers to help beautify the historic downtown. Their dream was to turn this dying factory town into a picturesque Vermont village like Woodstock and attract the tourists on their way to the ski resorts.

The man left to go inside and she procrastinated over one last cigarette. A few more moments of quiet while she gave herself a pep talk. It was a tiny gallery and she knew it would be crowded. Even worse, she would be walking in alone. All she could do was hold her head high and hope she didn't embarrass herself.

It was every bit as packed as she

feared. She made her way along, pretending to show great interest in the pieces up for silent auction. She didn't have much money and wasn't expecting to bid on anything. The displays being oohed and aahed over just reinforced to her that she knew so little about the subject. Most of it looked if not ugly then at least unappealing. After several minutes a small matted painting caught her eye. She thought her children might enjoy it so she placed a bid. She already knew that if she became the owner she would never get around to having it framed. She didn't know art but she did know herself.

After completing her round she went down the steps and entered the space outfitted for drinking champagne while the auction bids were sorted. There were several large tables that were already filled with the Important Wives and their Important Husbands. She recognized many of them, including some of her neighbors. She smiled but they did not smile back. Was that a sneer? She thinks that may have been a sneer. She hoped that her face wasn't turning as red as it felt like it was. She made her way to a small empty table near a window and waited to be served her champagne. Why did she think she could do this? Why did she think she should? Her address alone would not make them accept her. No doubt by the end of the evening her neighbors would have passed the gossip to their friends that she was living with an older lesbian and not an Important Husband. Her choice to attend was a mistake. The realization that she wouldn't want to fit in with this crowd landed a bit too late. Their dream of turning the town into another Woodstock wasn't about making it a better place for the rest of the residents. Not the people living in the crappy apartments on lower Main St. Or the folks living in one of the several low income housing developments. They wanted the town to look better so that *they* would look better. She didn't belong here. The young woman hired to pass out the champagne gave her a knowing smile. She smiled back in solidarity and thanked her sincerely. She sipped her champagne and stared out the window at the passing cars until the results of the auction were announced. The item was hers and she went back to the main room to settle the payment. No more classy fundraisers for her. She never did get the painting framed, either.

Kintsugi

The Kintsugi meme appeared in Kay's Facebook feed again and she sighed. The lovely bowl with its cracks repaired with gold made its way around social media a few times a year. She thought she may have even shared it herself the first time she saw it pop up. It was an inspirational concept and she had known people it certainly applied to, ones who had turned their damage into something beautiful to behold, but that wasn't her.

Kay's broken pieces are not beautiful. Time has polished and softened the edges of some, like potsherds found in the freshly tilled soil of cornfields along a riverbank. Reduced to evidence of the life lived long before. Other pieces are very much still jagged and sharp and continue to cause her pain. She tries her best to keep them from cutting those around her but sometimes she fails.

Her cracks are not filled with gold but with scar tissue. White and gnarled and constant reminders that the past will never go away. She was assured as a child that they would fade and disappear as she got older but she was lied to about many things. The only scars that faded from the view of others were the wounds that were properly tended to. She looks at her oddly flawless wrists and remembers the sensation of the tears burning behind her eyes as the emergency room nurse applied the sutures and bandages. Not tears of pain but of frustration. She couldn't do anything right. A mere half inch away the scars began again in earnest, running up both arms. Running straight through her soul.

She examines her broken pieces. Maybe her damage could have been beautiful if she had been a lovely bowl to begin with.

Rich

She sat at her desk and smiled to herself as the phone rang. She answered with the required professional greeting and tried to focus on the irate customer's account information but it was hard. She and Rich had an exceptionally good night last night and she was still glowing. She felt like the luckiest woman on Earth.

Have you ever met someone and knew instantly that it was meant to be? Rich said their romance was written in the stars. Yes, there was that time they argued but it was years ago and only happened once. He came back and she forgave him. It just made them grow closer.

At lunchtime she removed her chicken salad from the breakroom refrigerator and headed to the parking lot. She preferred to eat in her car and be alone with her thoughts. To think about Rich and try to imagine what he was doing at that moment. She ate in the breakroom once but found the gossip and chatter to be unbearable. She didn't want to hear about their plans for the holidays or what their children were doing now. She and Rich had decided early on never to have children. Rich would be a wonderful father but he said that their relationship was all they needed. They didn't need kids or friends or any family. They had each other and that was more than enough. She knew her coworkers thought she was antisocial and weird but she simply did not care about their lives. Besides, they didn't seem to be as happy as she was. What could she even contribute to the conversation? If she talked about Rich they might be jealous. Most people could only dream about having a love like theirs.

She returned to her desk and was just finishing up a call when her boss appeared in the doorway to ask her to stay for the next shift. He always asked her because he knew she didn't have a family to attend to and she would always say yes. Rich didn't mind. He wasn't controlling like so many other men. She would call him and let him know but she could already hear him laugh and say,"We can't survive on love alone." That was his standard response to her working late.

She understood intellectually that Rich wasn't perfect but her heart knew that he was perfect for her. He was so smart and sweet and funny. He told her often that she was beautiful even though the rest of the world had told her she wasn't. She remembered the teasing that occurred during her school years. The names she was called. The boy who asked her to go to prom while his friends looked on and laughed. But Rich did his best to help her push those memories away. His love was like a magic potion and she was happy to drown in it. To drown in *him*.

When she arrived home it was dark and Rich was already in the bedroom waiting for her. She hurried through her bedtime routine to join him, exhausted from her day but always ready for his love. She snuggled in so he could pull her close. She felt the familiar wetness and sighed. She stopped noticing the smell long ago but she couldn't stand the wet stage. In the morning she would wrap him in the waterproof mattress pad and drag him to the ditch out back. She would worry about replacing the fly strips after work. Maybe Saturday night she would check out the new bar up by the interstate. During last call Rich will approach her and ask if he can buy her a drink. Just like he always does.

Buttermilk Falls

It was 1977 when they moved into the rundown trailer on the dead end road that at some point in the distant past used to be a busy thoroughfare. It was the sort of trailer that poor people with few options lived in but right across the narrow empty road was magic.

There was a pull off into the woods that could hold a vehicle or two and beyond was a river that contained 3 sets of waterfalls. Quite the kingdom for a five year old who was very rarely supervised. Any actual attempt at safety consisted of being instructed not to enter the water without someone with her and she mostly remembered. It was difficult on the hot quiet mornings and, besides, standing in the river and letting the minnows nibble at her toes didn't really count, did it?

The Lower Falls were used primarily for fishing so she rarely ventured down there. One of her brothers had pulled out a 14 inch rainbow trout and it spooked her. She didn't want a fish that large deciding to see what she tasted like. It was still beautiful, though.

People swam at the Middle Falls but it required working your way over slippery rocks around the shallow edges to get to the parts deep enough for proper swimming. That is, unless you were brave enough to jump right in off of the overhanging ledge which she was not. Even during the hottest part of the summer the water was shockingly cold. She preferred to ease her way in, letting her body adjust as she went along. The Middle Falls was also most likely to have the naked people. She didn't mind them and they never spoke to her. She just pretended they weren't there.

The Upper Falls was the most popular hangout. It had a series of ledges that looked like they were carved out for the purpose of sitting or lounging. And the waterfall itself was like something out of a movie. You could swim over and sit or stand underneath it as the water came down. There was no hidden cave behind it but there should have been.

Above the Upper Falls was the most family friendly swimming hole and it was simply called The Bridge as it was beneath the first of the two dilapidated bridges that had caused the road to be closed. It had a small sandy beach and the best ledges for jumping or, for the brave or inebriated, diving. Even she would jump off of the lower ledge. It felt alarmingly high to her small five year old self but she would plunge straight down and feel her toes brush the rocks on the bottom.

But she didn't just love the river. There was a well worn path through the woods that ran from the Middle Falls up to The Bridge and that was where she spent most of her time. It wasn't what would be considered a comfortable walking trail for a kid. It had spots that required a bit of climbing with dips and hills and swarms of mosquitoes that threatened to carry her off but she loved it just the same. When she was by herself she could escape into her imagination where no one mistreated her. Maybe she could become an elf or fairy and never have to go home. Her bare feet alternating between toes gripping the rock ledges as she climbed or silently running along the pine needle covered packed earth. Investigating the roots of ancient trees that had been blown over by storms before her time. Watching the beetles burrowing their way into the soft, rotting wood. The appearance and consistency of the wood reminded her of cooked chicken and she thought that perhaps that was why the bugs seemed to enjoy eating it so much.

Sometimes hippies camped in the woods. She didn't know what the word 'hippies' meant but her parents used it in such a way that it suggested they should be looked down upon. As if somehow they could be lower than her family. This made her angry because they had been nothing but kind to her. They even shared their food sometimes. The danger to her existed within the cheaply paneled walls of her home so it didn't occur to her to be scared of the strangers, even if sometimes they did behave a bit oddly. She didn't know about drugs at that point or it would have made much more sense to her.

Years later she returned with her oldest child to introduce her to the wonders. The trailer was long gone. To her dismay she realized that her childhood kingdom looked very different through a caring mother's eyes. In place of adventure she saw the potential for sprained ankles or head injuries. And are those men over there drinking beer? She wondered how many they had consumed. As a 22 year old woman with a 4 year old daughter she suddenly felt it wasn't safe for them there. She hurried them back to the car and locked the doors before turning the key in the ignition. The magic was all gone. There was nothing there for her now.

Monsters

There was a loud knock at the front door. They never had visitors on their back road so the little girl's curiosity got the better of her and she crept partway down the stairs to eavesdrop. It was a sheriff and something horrible had happened. Less than two miles away a woman and her daughters had been attacked inside their home. They were dead. He dropped his voice a bit as he added,"And appear to have been violated."

He asked her mother if she had seen anything. She said she had been out in the garden until just a little while before and hadn't noticed anything. He warned her to lock the doors and stay inside, at least until morning, and to call the police if she saw anything out of the ordinary.

"I will, sheriff," she assured him. "My daughter and I are here alone and this is terrifying."

Her mother closed the door and there followed the sound of the rarely used lock clicking into place. After waiting for him to climb in his truck and drive away she unlocked it and headed back into the kitchen to continue cooking their supper. The little girl's stomach rolled. She wondered how young the daughters were. Her stomach rolled again. Where could she hide? Not her bedroom. That wasn't safe. Her closet was useless. It was tiny and had no door. Under the bed was out of the question as everyone knows that's the first place the bad guys always look. Just last week her teacher punished her for having a grownup horror novel in her desk but she didn't have the words to explain that haunted houses and ghosts were the fun kind of scary. Real people were much scarier. They were the true monsters. The odor of the browning meat was making her feel even more nauseated. How could she possibly eat? Her mother would be angry with her like she usually was at mealtimes. She felt trapped so she continued to sit on the stairs. And she waited.

What felt like an eternity later her father and brothers came home. The woman who gave birth to her smiled as she instructed them to throw their bloody clothes in the washer and clean themselves up because supper was almost ready. They were having goulash.

The little girl sat on the stairs quietly and waited to be called to the table.

On the Acquisition of Food

The email came in telling her that the grocery order was ready. She peeked out the window before opening the door because she really didn't feel like running into her neighbors. They seemed like nice enough people but she wasn't up for empty small talk. The coast was clear so she headed for the car.

Once buckled in she put her foot on the brake and pressed the ignition button. For the millionth time she wondered what the point was. Why replace the good ol' key in the ignition? It still required a key anyway. A key whose battery wears out and leaves you panicking in a parking lot away from home. They had purchased the car over 4 years before and she still missed the old car. The old car that was the same make and style as the one before and the one before that. Her autistic brain just wasn't fond of change.

She waited for all the electronic nonsense to kick in. She could pull out immediately but she wanted to make sure the music was right first. It had to be *the* song. The same song she had been playing on a loop in the car for the past 5 months. Ah, now the touchscreen is telling her to drive safely. What would she do without it? Here she had been planning on flying down the hill all willy-nilly and blowing through the intersection with no regard for the lights but fortunately the car reminded her not to. Stupid car. Just play the fucking song.

There it is. Now she can go. It was less than a mile to the grocery store. More than enough time to get anxious. What if someone ran a red light and slammed into her? What if all of the assigned curbside parking spots were taken by people who were in the store shopping and then she had to call the store to explain where she was parked?

She already knew the substitutions and out of stock items but what if they forgot to include something in her order? They forgot something once, months ago, so of course now it was a constant concern.

Down the hill and through the intersection unscathed but she still had to make it back. Two of the curbside spots were taken but she was able to park in the third and now came the wait. Time to count masks. Her county was listed as having high community spread but few people seemed to care. She spotted a couple masks, both on shoppers who looked to be in their seventies. It bothered her that those at highest risk were the least likely to be able to access the curbside pickup since it required a computer or smartphone.

In the side mirror she spotted a familiar woman pulling the familiar yellow cart so she cracked her window and popped the trunk. The workers were so used to seeing her that they never asked for a name anymore but they would still make polite noises at her. She opened her mouth and heard the standard polite responses come out. It was a scripted exchange and she got her part right this time. All she had to do now was make it back home and carry the groceries into the house.

Shit. She pulled into their parking spot right after the neighbor pulled into hers. It would take the woman a few minutes to get the kids in the house so she pretended to be busy checking something on her phone. She was too tired to make any more polite mouth noises today. She hoped they hurried before the ice cream started to melt. Melty ice cream was almost as bad as having to talk to people. They were nearing their door so she could start the process of transferring the food to the house. Frozen stuff first and cheese balls last. She was exhausted but if she played her cards right it would be 3-4 days before she had to do it all over again. Same food order. Same song. Same routine. Same anxiety.

He Never Beat Her

"Matt won't come over anymore. He doesn't like you."

Rachel felt like her organs had been ripped out of her torso and went into the other room to cry. She knew she could be awkward and say stupid shit sometimes but, try as she might, she couldn't remember a single embarrassing thing she may have said or done in his presence. Matt was a nice guy and she liked him. He was calm and soft spoken so it didn't stress her out when he would come visit her husband. They would sit at the kitchen table, drinking and talking for a few hours, while she and the baby stayed out of their hair.

Her husband came from a large Catholic family and, at 38, was one of the younger siblings. Most of her in-laws treated her like a stupid child. It annoyed her but she also understood. After all, she was 18 and some of them had kids her age or even a few years older. She was a joke to them.

Matt and his wife were different, though. They were always very kind to her. One time his wife came by when Rachel was pregnant and told her to leave and not give the baby her brother's name. She said he only wanted a young woman to train and that he would take the baby if she tried to leave later. Rachel made an attempt to argue with her but didn't really know what to say. She wouldn't admit it to her but she knew that what her sister in-law said was true because he had already begun threatening to take away their child after it was born. She was scared and had nowhere to go.

Over the next few years she would wonder what she had done to make Matt no longer want to visit but life went on and she was busy with being a mom. It was never too far from her mind, though. She had believed that Matt liked her and if she could be so wrong about him, who else was she wrong about? *What* else was she wrong about? She felt like she must be crazy.

Her husband wanted her to stay home but she began to want some independence. She had a roof over her head and food to eat but she wanted her own money. It felt degrading when she would have to ask for a dollar if she wanted to go have a cup of coffee at Friendly's with her sister. He acted like she was being unreasonable. When they would argue he would remind her that he was a good husband because he didn't beat her. She would doubt herself and think that maybe she *was* unreasonable. It's not like he was abusing her.

An older friend offered to teach her how to drive and then sell her the car she learned on for $500. He seemed oddly okay with that but there were conditions. He told her she would have to find a job and a babysitter that she could walk to because he wouldn't help her buy the car. He said they didn't have the money and since she wasn't allowed to know their finances, she believed him. At least until he purchased a $500 stereo for his 12 year old son. That stung but she did her best to not let on. Since he didn't want her working he wouldn't help with the childcare expenses, either. Why wouldn't she just be happy with staying home? She had no education and little experience so the best she could do was a minimum wage factory job and after taxes and child care it didn't leave her with much. She was able to work overtime and save up the money to buy the car but she was so burnt out from the added hours and lack of sleep that she was forced to quit. This pleased him but she was determined to recoup and try again.

The harder she tried to work the more she kept burning out. He told her repeatedly that she was lazy and she believed him. It would be decades before she learned she was autistic and that burning out was unfortunately common.

After 5 years she did end up leaving. As expected he threatened to keep their child and by that point she was so broken mentally that she agreed to not fight for custody in exchange for generous visitation rights.

Several years later she would bring their child down to see the sister in-law who had been so kind. During that visit she mustered up the courage to ask what she had done to make Matt dislike her so much that he wouldn't come back. She was prepared to be hurt again but her former sister in-law was angry as she explained that the issue was never Rachel herself. Matt had come home from that final visit furious because her husband had drunkenly knocked his glass off the table and ordered Rachel to clean up the mess. She had been lied to about Matt disliking her. He stopped coming back because he couldn't stomach seeing her treated that way. All those years of wondering what she did wrong and it turned out to be an incident so commonplace that Rachel didn't even remember it.

In a perfect world that would have eased Rachel's mind but there were too many years of feeling stupid and lazy and unlikable to be erased. 30 years later those feelings still persist. But he was a good husband because he never beat her.

The Photograph

It is a black and white photo of a weathered barn. Many such pictures exist but none like this. This one is special. It is a portal to multiple realities. It is a slice outside of time captured through the loving eye of an angel. In the foreground is a light that you would expect to see on a television or film set. The composition of the image is such that the lamp appears to be directing your attention to the barn that is back there. As if it is saying,"Yes, I am here but look there. The barn is *significant.*"

I have never been inside this barn. It is 1,100 miles away but looking at the image instantly transports me through time and space. I can hear the swallows that have built their mud nests in the rafters and the humming vibration of the summer heat that is as much a physical sensation as it is a sound. My nose is filled with the odor of hay and the dust motes that float in the air and I sneeze. Now I'm on a hay wagon and the men are shouting back and forth to each other as they work. I am far too small to toss the bails but I can stack them. The heat of the sun is intense but I hardly notice as I am too happy to be there. A stubborn child struggling to prove my worth. Struggling to prove that girls are good for more than what the men in my mother's life wanted them for. One of them laughs as he tosses up a bail that contains the remains of a snake that did not move fast enough. He expects me to be scared but instead my heart hurts. I like snakes and the only disgust I feel is for his callousness.

Death. I'm no longer nine. Now it is 2011 and there is the barn on my television screen. It doesn't smell of hay but of death. Death and grief and terror at the way the world changed for the characters we had begun to love. It was all make-believe then but it doesn't feel so much now that the real world has changed, too.

The photo is magic mixed with love. It is art within art. It is a snapshot of what was and what always will be. And it's so beautiful that it makes my heart ache.

Salad

It felt like forever since the world shut down and she wasn't sure what to do with herself. She had already binged everything that appealed to her on Netflix and Amazon. There was always her DVD collection if she got desperate enough. It was rather extensive and went back 20 years. She remembered how easily one could stroll into a store and purchase whatever movie struck their fancy. Or their preferred toilet paper brand. She was covered on that for now, though. The store she ordered her groceries from had been out of stock but she found some paper for RV toilets online. Didn't love it but it was better than nothing. She heard people were getting bidets. That seemed a bit extreme to her, not that her landlord would allow one if she decided to try that route. How did the whole bidet thing work anyway? Wouldn't they require you to dry afterwards with ass towels? If you have ass towels to wash every time you do your business then why not just use damp face cloths? Although, she supposed they would be called ass cloths in that case. With all the conspiracy theories flying around online she was surprised no one had suggested the virus was cooked up in a lab by Big Bidet. She suddenly had the urge to write a Facebook post to that effect and time how quickly it took her aunt to share it as fact. Nah. Then the rest of her family would get mad at her. Again. She sighed.

She was bored. Really bored. Other people had hobbies but she was never much of a hobby person. Normally she would be reading but her concentration had disappeared along with her freedom of movement. Not that she was a big fan of the outside world anyway but she did miss the ability to choose whether she interacted with it or not. And what was with the sourdough bread? She wasn't much of a baker or cook but if she had been she didn't think she would spend her time on a baked good that she didn't enjoy eating in the first place.

She was suddenly lonely. She tried to remember the last time someone hugged her and couldn't. It was a while before the virus upended everything. When was the last time she even got laid? Oh, that's right. After her cousin's wedding reception. Some guy named Gary. Or was it Barry? Wait. It was Ryan. How the hell did she confuse the names Gary and Ryan? It was a mediocre experience anyway. She thought about the cucumber that had been in the grocery order delivered this morning. What the fuck? She must be losing her mind. The cucumber is for the salad she planned to have for supper. She had eaten entirely too much ice cream in the past few weeks so she was making an effort to eat healthier. Again. Is it still called supper if she ends up staying awake all night and eats it at

7am or is a 7am meal referred to as 'breakfast' by default? What if time no longer holds any meaning? At least she knew it was Wednesday. Wednesday was Grocery Delivery Day.

The woman in the apartment across the street was out on her balcony tending to her little garden. Along with baking sourdough bread everyone was also taking up gardening. She wished she had a balcony so she could try gardening. Maybe she would enjoy it. There was always hydroponic gardening although her landlord might get twitchy about that ever since the guy on the 5th floor had the fish tank mishap. That was a mess. Then again, the landlord wasn't exactly dropping by to check up on his tenants these days. She considered googling to see how hard it was. Could one grow cucumbers hydroponically? Oh my God. Stop thinking about cucumbers.

She wished she could open some windows. The weather was getting beautiful out and she would love some fresh air but then the sounds of the ambulance sirens would be louder. They were upsetting enough with the windows closed. She tried not to think about it. The waves of panic were bad enough when she tried to sleep. No use in being an anxious mess during the day, too. Knitting and crocheting were out. Tried them both when she was younger and hated them. Painting? No talent. She missed reading. Her best friends were books and she no longer had them to comfort her, either. How was she going to make it through the rest of the day? She could do laundry but then she should shower. She hadn't showered since, wait, she wasn't even sure. What day is it? Wednesday. Today is Wednesday but it's pronounced 'wensday'. Why didn't they just spell it 'Wensday'? Then there's 'February'. And silent Ks. She sighed again. Next week she will order two cucumbers.

Marlboro Light

She didn't like Phil. He scared her so she avoided him and didn't speak to him unless she absolutely had to. The others worshiped him like he was some kind of god but her first week there he had gotten angry and threw a chair across the room so she didn't trust him. He always wore wife beaters that showed off the gunshot scar on his shoulder and cussed like a sailor. The others told her that he used to be a bouncer and got shot during a bar fight. It just added to their awe. She couldn't understand why a man like that was allowed to work with vulnerable kids.

Earlier that night she had broken the mirror in her compact to use the glass to hurt herself. Seven years of bad luck. How many mirrors had she already broken for this purpose? Times seven? She was doomed until the day she died. But she had gone too far and the staff on duty decided she needed stitches. Phil offered to be the one to take her.

They climbed into the van and rode in silence. He lit one of the Marlboro lights that he was always smoking and held it out to her. Was this a trap? She was only 13 and the facility's rules clearly stated that anyone under the age of 14 caught smoking would receive restrictions. She had already been busted for smoking a few times and the restrictions would be increased. It had been a rough night and she could really use a cigarette but she still hesitated.

"Take it before I change my mind."

She took it and inhaled deeply. It helped take a bit of the edge off. She had never been to a big city emergency room. She didn't like noise or crowded waiting rooms but she had no one else to blame for her predicament. She had really fucked up this time.

Phil had called ahead and they got her into a curtained off examination area surprisingly fast. They didn't speak as they waited for someone to come examine her wound. She went away in her head and imagined she was anywhere else. Finally a nurse came in with supplies but before she could begin to use them all hell broke loose. There had been a serious car accident with multiple victims. The nurse disappeared like a flash and the waiting began again.

After what felt like an eternity she noticed that Phil was doing something odd with his feet. He would lift a foot up exaggeratingly high and then set it back down in a different position. Then he would do it with his other foot. Over and over. What the hell? Then it hit her. Anyone looking towards the curtain would just see the feet coming down, every which way. She began to laugh. The absurdity of it in the midst of such a stressful situation made it too funny not to. She imagined what it must look like from the outside and laughed even harder. He looked pleased with himself and said softly,"You're going to be okay."

Shortly thereafter the nurse returned to quickly apply some Steri-strips. She apologized for the substandard treatment but said that they had too much going on and didn't want us to be stuck there all night. The wound really was too large for them to work and the strips came off within 24 hours but another scar didn't really matter.

She was still wary of Phil but that faded with time. The vast majority of the kids at the facility were boys and she could see where his tough guy act came in handy at certain points. Months later she recounted his emergency room antics to one of the other staff members and they said,"He's rough but he would die for any of you kids," and she believed them.

Decades later and she still can't see a Marlboro light without thinking of him and that night.

Bad Penny

The little boy admired the shiny new penny. He tilted it this way and that in the glow of his flashlight under his makeshift blanket tent. His grandpa handed it to him earlier that night, with a wink and a grin as his mother was looking the other way. It was their little secret but the kind of secret that made him feel nice inside. Not like the secrets that his uncle made him keep. Not the secrets that made him feel bad. Like *he* was bad. He carefully placed the penny under his pillow and turned off the flashlight to settle in to sleep. Maybe the magic of the shiny new penny would keep the nightmares away for one night.

By morning it was clear that the penny wasn't magic but it could still be useful. After lunch he announced he was going out to play and headed to the little store on the corner. They had penny candy and he had already decided on which one he wanted by the time he arrived. One Pixy Stix later and the penny was in the till.

Other customers came and went but the penny remained in the till, simply by chance, as the bored clerk continued to scoop out change for purchases. Until the young man bought two bottles of Coke and a pack of Camels. The penny made its way into the pocket of the young man's cleanest jeans. It was Saturday and his boss at the garage let him borrow a car to take his girlfriend out that night. He wasn't sure if she was really his girl yet but she was pretty enough for now. More importantly, she was as poor as he was so didn't mind that he couldn't take her anywhere fancy. Going for a drive and drinking Cokes by the lake would be enough.

Dusk found them in the backseat of the old Buick where he assured her that it would be okay. He told her that he loved her, and in that moment he may have even believed it himself. The jeans ended up on the floor and the penny slipped out and landed just under the driver's seat where it remained until long after they found out that, no, it wouldn't be okay. Their parents raged and cried and then marriage happened.

Helping out at the garage was not enough to support his new family. He was desperate and decided that joining the military was his best option. He knew he would be sent to war and he knew that men like him were dying but maybe he would be one of the lucky ones and survive. His wife and child stayed with her family. They never saw him again.

Seven years, 2 months, and 23 days later a man was at the junkyard scavenging for useful things when he came across the old Buick. During the once-over he discovered the penny. It was in mint condition for a 1965 coin and he briefly considered setting it aside but he wasn't that kind of man. Money is money so he stuck it in his pocket with the rest of the coins he had acquired that day. He stopped by the Wagon Wheel for a few beers on his way home where he would later punch his wife in the chest for daring to rebuff his drunken advances.

The penny spent a while bouncing around town. Back to the corner store. On to the gas station. Reunited with the Wagon Wheel's bartender. Mr Graham's fatal heart attack. Mrs Hammer's miscarriage. Little Jenny's drowning. Around and around it went. No one noticed because why would they have? Such is the incestuous nature of small towns.

The salesman stopped at the gas station on his way through. He had gotten a bit lost but before long he was back on track and heading home to Bakersfield. He had been gone for several weeks but it was worth it as his trip was quite successful. He talked his wife into leaving the kids with his mother while they celebrated with a weekend in

L.A. He had guilt about the night he spent with the waitress in Des Moines. In the end it didn't matter because his wife had her guilt, too. It would be a little over 6 years before he would find out that his youngest son wasn't actually his.

The penny continued its journey around the City of Angels. Dreams stolen away, breast cancer, the young runaway who killed herself because she was tired of trading sex to predatory men for a safe place to sleep.

The penny never encountered any movie stars. The closest it came to fame was the 17 days it spent in the possession of a monster named Ken Bianchi. Ken did horrible things with the help of his monstrous older cousin. The penny traveled with him to Washington state where he wanted to prove to his cousin that he could do horrible things without him. It had already found its way to a nightclub by the time Ken was arrested.

The little girl spotted the penny on the sidewalk as she and her mother hurried to the bus stop in the cold drizzle.

“Stop, mommy! A penny!”

“Leave it be, sweetie. Tails up means bad luck.” And they lived happily ever after.

www.ingramcontent.com/pod-product-compliance
Lightning Source LLC
LaVergne TN
LVHW050327160826
845677LV00014B/3554

* 9 7 9 8 8 4 6 6 9 4 2 8 6 *